100
YEARS OF
RUGBY

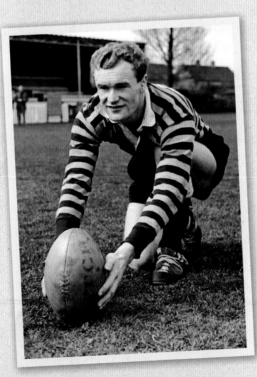

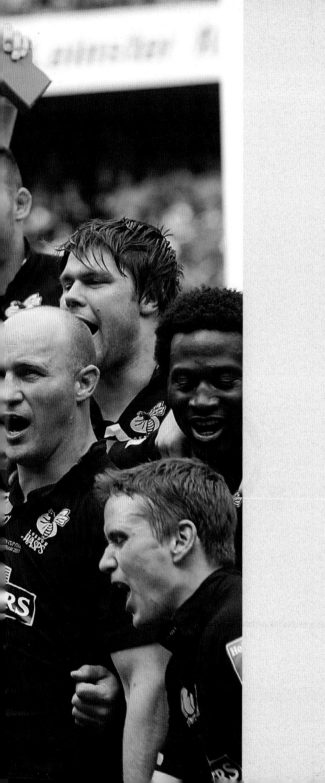

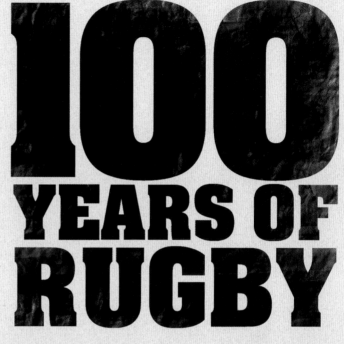

100
YEARS OF
RUGBY

PA Photos

AMMONITE
PRESS

First published 2008 by

AMMONITE PRESS

an imprint of AE Publications Ltd,

166 High Street, Lewes, East Sussex BN7 1XU

ISBN 978-1-906672-02-7

Editor **NEIL DUNNICLIFFE**
Designer **JO PATTERSON**

Colour origination by GMC Reprographics
Printed and bound by Colorprint Offset in China

Contents

Chapter One
PEOPLE

THE GREAT AND GOOD

It is the big personalities that make rugby so exciting

In the beginning there was William Webb Ellis. Or *perhaps* there was. The story that he picked up the ball and ran with it at Rugby School in 1823 may be just that: a story. All over the UK there were already games in existence which involved running with a ball, and throwing it – it just didn't happen in a game of football, which Ellis allegedly tried.

But whatever happened, the first rugby rules were written down in 1845. Prior to that the competing teams would have to agree which rules they were playing by before they kicked off. So by the time the 20th century arrived, the basic rules of rugby were over half a century old and the Rugby Football Union had been born in 1871.

JEHOIDA HODGES, WALES.
10/01/1908

It was also in 1871 that the first international, between England and Scotland, was played – with Scotland winning. By 1886 there was an International Rugby Board and by 1895 the split with the professionals of what would become Rugby League had taken place. By 1900 rugby in the UK as we know it today had essentially arrived, complete with a Four Nations Championship.

EARLY DAYS

Even the name of the England captain for the 1905 Four Nations Championship, Frank Stout, harks back to a different era. And there's the splendidly named Welsh international Jehoida Hodges of Newport. In 1903, playing England at Swansea, Hodges was hauled out of the pack to replace his injured Welsh Captain, Tom Pearson, on the left wing. He scored a hat-trick, and two years later played for Wales when they beat the All Blacks. It was the only defeat the New Zealanders suffered on their first ever tour of the British Isles and France. It was also, interestingly, the tour on which the New Zealanders discovered the break-away game of Rugby League being played in the north of England.

It was against Wales that Wavell Wakefield made his English debut, in 1920. Wakefield was to become one of the game's leading figures in the 1920s, and for many years after. He was President of the RFU in 1950, became an MP and was knighted to become Baron Wakefield of Kendal. Wakefield served in the Royal Naval Air Service during World War One, was an accomplished cricketer and sprinter, and helped England to Grand Slam wins in 1921, 1923 and 1924. He also captained England in 13 of his 31 internationals, a record which was only broken by Bill Beaumont in the 1980s.

One of the game's characters in the 1930s was undoubtedly Prince Alexander Sergeevich Obolensky. Known as 'Obo' or 'The Prince', Obolensky was a Russian Prince who fled Russia after the Revolution in 1917 and ended up in Muswell Hill. He made his England debut in January 1936, a controversial choice as he only became a British citizen a few months after the match. It was a scintillating performance, though, and his two

tries helped beat the All Blacks 13-0. His first effort, which involved him running almost the length of the pitch, is still talked of as one of the greatest England tries of all time. When World War Two broke out the Prince joined the RAF, and was killed in 1940 at the age of just 24.

Wilfred Wooller was one of the greatest ever Welsh all-rounders. He won 18 rugby caps for Wales – the first of these was gained while Wooler was still at school – captained Glamorgan at cricket for 14 years, and once scored a hat-trick playing centre forward for Cardiff City.

WILF WOOLLER, CAMBRIDGE UNIVERSITY AND WALES. 18/01/1936

LEAGUE AND UNION

It was the vexed question of earning a living that caused the 1895 split which led to there being two rugby nations in the British Isles – League and Union. Players like Lewis Jones, Jonathan Davies, Alan Tait and Scott Gibbs excelled at both games and won international caps in both sports, but with the professionalisation of Rugby Union in 1995 – exactly 100 years after the original split – the flow of players was reversed.

A lot of the animosity was lost too, as players and fans began to respect what both codes had to offer.

One overwhelming success who switched from League to Union was Jason Robinson. While he was playing in league his astonishing acceleration earned him the nickname Billy Whizz, after the fast-moving cartoon character in The Beano. Although he had won 19 caps for England and Great

Britain as a League player, there were still raised eyebrows when he was picked to play for the England team in February 2001, only three months after he had made his club debut with Sale Sharks. The eyebrows went even higher, though, when people saw what Robinson could do. He was one of the most exciting players to have donned the England jersey, and one of those great players who quicken the pulse every time they get the ball.

LEFT
WALES' ALLAN MARTIN (C) WINS
THE BALL AT A LINE OUT.
05/03/1977

OPPOSITE BELOW
ENGLAND'S JONNY WILKINSON
KEEPS AN EYE ON THE SCRUM.
03/02/2007

OPPOSITE ABOVE
ENGLAND'S LAWRENCE
DALLAGLIO. 06/10/2007

HEADLINE MAKERS

The only player in recent years to grab more headlines than Jason Robinson has been Jonny Wilkinson. Like those stars of a century ago, Wilkinson excelled at several sports and would probably have succeeded at cricket if the lives of modern-day sports stars didn't demand a full-time focus on one game only.

For Wilkinson it had to be rugby, which he had played since he was four. On an under-18s tour of Australia he scored 94 points in five matches, and he has scored more than 1000 test match points for England.

Scotland's Scott Murray had an

unusual introduction to rugby, but has gone on to become his country's most capped player. Murray was a schools international basketball

player when a rugby coach spotted his 6'6" frame as he was working in a supermarket. He played twice for Scotland in the 2007 Rugby World Cup and, presumably, has no plans to go back to supermarket shelves.

Neil Jenkins has scored more than 1000 test match points for Wales. The players of a century ago would have shaken their heads in disbelief at such figures, as one or two test matches a year was the norm. Rugby has definitely come a long way!

ENGLAND TEAM GROUP. 13/03/1886

WALES TEAM GROUP. 05/01/1895

EDWARD TEMPLE GURDON,

RICHMOND. 1895

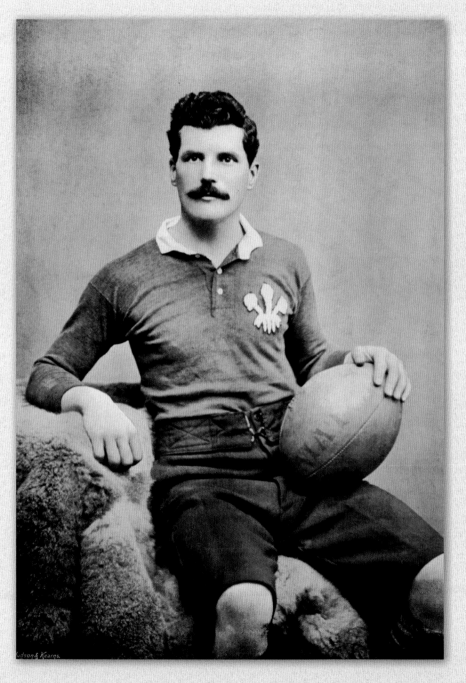

ARTHUR GOULD, WALES. 1895

CAMBRIDGE UNIVERSITY TEAM 1913-14. 01/10/1913

(L-R) W.J.A. 'DAVE' DAVIES AND CECIL
KERSHAW, UNITED SERVICES.
01/04/1920

CAMBRIDGE UNIVERSITY CAPTAIN
GEOFFREY CONWAY (C) INTRODUCES
HIS TEAM TO HM KING GEORGE V (L)
BEFORE THE LAST VARSITY MATCH TO
BE PLAYED AT QUEEN'S.
06/12/1920

SCOTLAND CAPTAIN PHIL MACPHERSON (HALF HIDDEN BEHIND KING) INTRODUCES HIS TEAM TO KING GEORGE VI
BEFORE THE MATCH AGAINST ENGLAND. 17/03/1930

CAMBRIDGE UNIVERSITY CAPTAIN J.J.A. EMBLETON LEADS HIS TEAM OUT AT TWICKENHAM. 18/10/1930

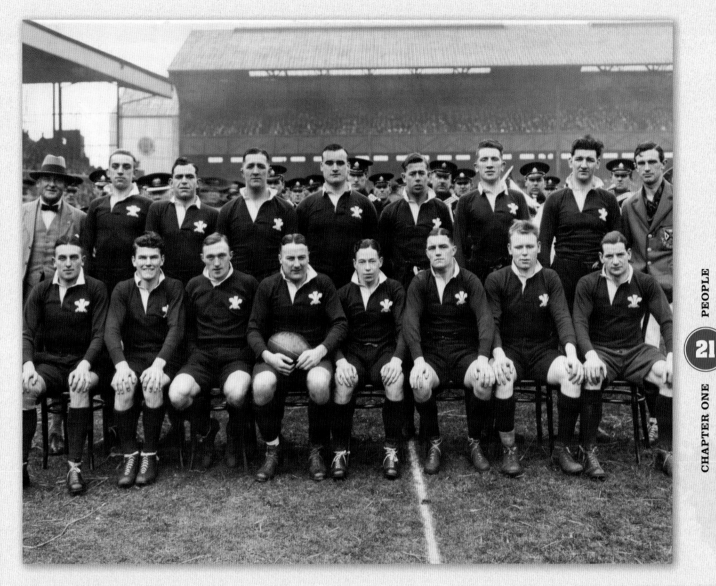

WALES TEAM GROUP. 17/01/1931

ALEXANDER SERGEEVICH OBOLENSKY (R) DIVES TO MAKE A TACKLE. 05/11/1937

SCOTLAND'S WILLIAM YOUNG (L) GRABS ENGLAND'S JIMMY GILES (R) BY THE LEG AS THE LATTER TRIES TO KICK TOWARDS THE POSTS. 19/03/1938

(L-R) C.S. BONGARD, RFU COMMITTEE MEMBER, AND BILLY WILLIAMS, PURCHASER OF THE LAND ON WHICH TWICKENHAM WAS BUILT. 10/11/1945

FRANCE'S LUCIEN CARON (C) PASSES THE BALL OUT AS HE IS TACKLED BY ENGLAND'S ROBERT KENNEDY (11). 26/02/1949

WALES' KEN JONES (L) SPRINTS FOR THE FRENCH TRY LINE. 25/03/1950

WALES' ROY JOHN WINS THE BALL AT A LINE OUT. 19/01/1952

WALES' DAI DAVIES (L) BRINGS DOWN ENGLAND'S GORDON RIMMER (R). 19/01/1952

SOUTH AFRICA'S FONNIE DU TOIT
WAVES GOODBYE WITH A BUNCH OF
MINI RUGBY BALLS AS HE BOARDS
THE TRAIN AT WATERLOO AT THE END
OF HIS TEAM'S TOUR. 21/02/1952

JEAN PRAT, FRANCE CAPTAIN, DURING A MATCH AGAINST ENGLAND. 28/02/1953

NEW ZEALAND FULL BACK BOB SCOTT
PRACTISES HIS KICKING AT THE
COLLEGE GROUNDS, EASTBOURNE.
22/10/1953

THE NEW ZEALAND SQUAD PRACTISE THEIR HAKA AT EASTBOURNE COLLEGE DURING THEIR TOUR OF THE NORTHERN HEMISPHERE. 23/10/1953

BRITISH LIONS CAPTAIN ROBIN THOMPSON (C), C. MEREDITH (L) AND D. WILSON (R). 06/06/1955

PETER YARRANTON. 17/11/1955

ENGLAND'S MUSCLES CURRIE (SECOND L) IS TACKLED BY SCOTLAND'S ROBERT MACEWEN (THIRD L). 16/03/1957

PETER ROBBINS, OXFORD UNIVERSITY
CAPTAIN. 21/11/1957

OPPOSITE
ITALIAN ACTRESS MILLY VITALE KICKS
OFF AS PLAYERS FROM BOTH TEAMS
LOOK ON. BLACKHEATH V MILAN XV.
23/11/1957

HRH THE DUKE OF GLOUCESTER (L) TALKS TO ENGLAND CAPTAIN ERIC EVANS (R) BEFORE THE MATCH. 01/02/1958

ERIC EVANS, ENGLAND CAPTAIN.
08/02/1958

LONDON COUNTIES CAPTAIN DICKIE JEEPS (R) GIVES A TACTICAL TALK DURING TRAINING. 11/11/1960

OPPOSITE

KEN SCOTLAND, HERIOT'S FORMER PUPILS AND SCOTLAND. 01/02/1960

PETER DAWKINS, AN AMERICAN AT OXFORD, GETTING AWAY WITH THE BALL AS HE IS ABOUT TO BE TACKLED BY D.F.B WRENCH OF CAMBRIDGE. 06/12/1960

IRELAND'S WILLIE-JOHN MCBRIDE (C) DROPS THE BALL AS HE IS TACKLED BY WALES' KEITH ROWLANDS. 09/03/1963

MODEL ROBINA LAKE WITH MEMBERS OF THE CATFORD BRIDGE RUGBY CLUB.   30/01/1964

MIKE GIBSON LINES UP A KICK DURING PRACTICE. 26/04/1966

TERRY PRICE, LLANELLI AND WALES.
01/07/1967

KEITH JARRETT, WALES. 19/01/1968

INJURED ENGLAND CAPTAIN DICK GREENWOOD (L) WITH HIS REPLACEMENT FOR THE FRANCE MATCH, BUDGE ROGERS (R), AT TRAINING. 21/02/1969

WALES CAPTAIN BRIAN PRICE LEADS HIS TEAM OUT. 08/03/1969

WALES SCRUM HALF GARETH EDWARDS FEEDS HIS BACKS. 07/02/1970

IRELAND'S TONY O'REILLY THROWS IN AT A LINE OUT AGAINST ENGLAND. 14/02/1970

WALES' MIKE ROBERTS (C) LAYS THE BALL BACK TO SCRUM HALF GARETH EDWARDS (9). 16/01/1971

WALES' MERVYN DAVIES (L) AND JOHN TAYLOR (R) COMBINE TO WIN THE LINE OUT BALL. 13/03/1971

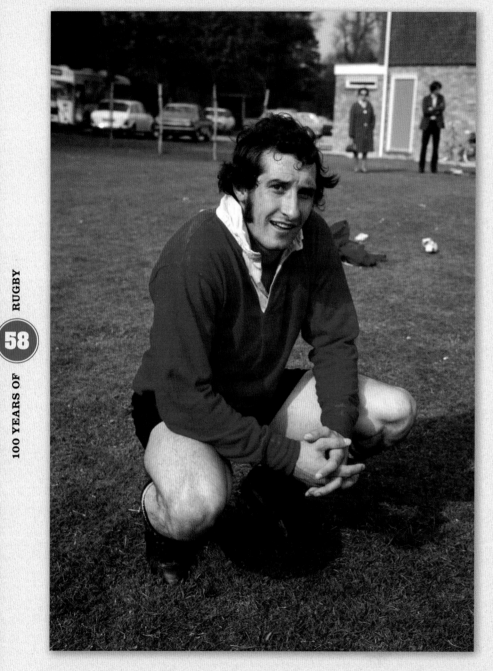

GARETH EDWARDS, WALES AND
BRITISH LIONS. 30/05/1971

JOHN TAYLOR, BRITISH LIONS AND
WALES. 31/05/1971

ENGLAND'S DAVID DUCKHAM TRIES TO OUTPACE THE REST. 01/01/1972

ENGLAND'S CHRIS RALSTON (C) WINS THE LINEOUT BALL. 26/02/1972

WALES SCRUM-HALF GARETH EDWARDS GETS THE BALL AWAY FROM A SCRUM. 15/03/1975

DANNY WILSON, CARDIFF (R). 17/01/1976

WALES' ALLAN MARTIN (C) WINS THE BALL AT A LINE OUT. 17/01/1976

BILL BEAUMONT, ENGLAND. 05/03/1977

ENGLAND'S NIGEL HORTON (C) WINS THE BALL AT A LINE OUT. 04/02/1978

ENGLAND CAPTAIN BILL BEAUMONT GIVES A TEAM TALK DURING TRAINING. 16/03/1978

J.P.R. WILLIAMS, WALES. 18/03/1978

ENGLAND'S TONY NEARY (C) TAKES ON FRANCE'S JEAN-LUC JOINEL (R) AND JEROME GALLION (L). 03/03/1979

DUSTY HARE KICKS A LAST MINUTE
PENALTY TO GIVE ENGLAND VICTORY
OVER WALES AT TWICKENHAM.
16/02/1980

ENGLAND'S STEVE SMITH (C) FEEDS HIS BACKS. 15/03/1980

ENGLAND CAPTAIN BILL BEAUMONT (HEADBAND) PASSES THE BALL AS HE IS TACKLED DURING THE CALCUTTA CUP MATCH AGAINST SCOTLAND AT TWICKENHAM. 21/02/1981

WALES' DICK MORIARTY (C) POWERS THROUGH THE AUSTRALIA DEFENCES. 05/12/1981

ROBERT PAPAREMBORDE, FRANCE, DURING A MATCH AGAINST WALES. 06/02/1982

GRAHAM PRICE, WALES. 06/02/1982

STEVE SMITH, ENGLAND CAPTAIN. 06/02/1983

ENGLAND'S JOHN CARLETON IS HELPED OFF THE PITCH AFTER BEING INJURED. 19/11/1983

THREE OF ENGLAND'S RUGBY HEROES, CONQUERORS OF THE NEW ZEALAND ALL-BLACKS AT TWICKENHAM, WHO REGISTERED A 15-9 WIN OVER THE TOURING SIDE, THE FIRST TIME THEY HAVE DONE THIS SINCE 1936. (L-R) CAPTAIN PETER WHEELER, CLIVE WOODWARD AND JOHN CARLETON. 15/12/1983

ENGLAND'S JON HALL (C) BREAKS AWAY FROM A SCRUM, ASSISTED BY DAVID COOKE (L) AND WATCHED BY WADE DOOLEY (R, BACKGROUND). 16/03/1985

ENGLAND'S PAUL ACKFORD (C) WINS
THE LINE OUT BALL UNDER
PRESSURE. 05/11/1988

NEW ZEALAND ALL BLACKS' WALTER LITTLE BREAKS CLEAR AGAINST PONTYPOOL. 18/10/1989

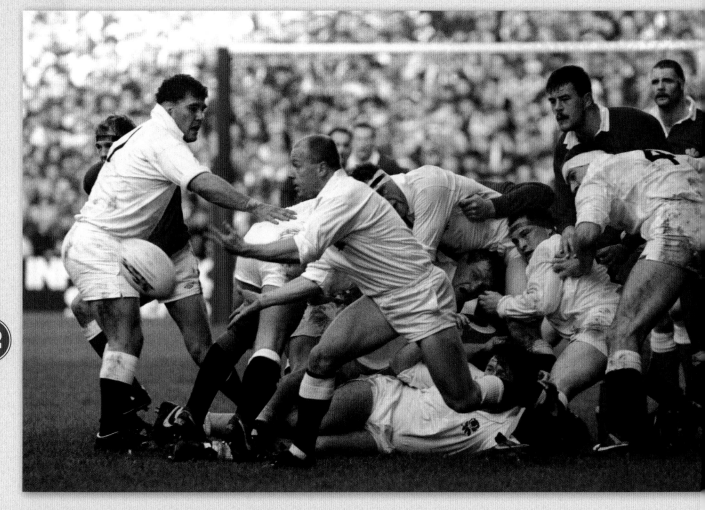

ENGLAND'S RICHARD HILL (C) FEEDS HIS BACKS FROM A SCRUM. 19/01/1991

GAVIN HASTINGS, SCOTLAND. 02/02/1991

JOHN MALLETT OF BATH, UPSET
AFTER BEING BEATEN BY WATERLOO
TO GO OUT OF THE PILKINGTON CUP.
28/11/1992

IEUAN EVANS, WALES. 06/02/1993

LEICESTER'S MARTIN JOHNSON WINS A LINE OUT BALL. 01/05/1993

MARTIN JOHNSON, BRITISH & IRISH LIONS. 16/06/1993

BRITISH & IRISH LIONS' BRIAN MOORE PRACTISES A LINE OUT THROW. 22/06/1993

JASON LEONARD (L) AND IEUAN EVANS (R) OF BRITISH LIONS CELEBRATE BEATING NEW ZEALAND IN THE SECOND TEST.
26/06/1993

NEIL BACK, LEICESTER TIGERS. 01/01/1994

VICTOR UBOGU, ENGLAND, KEEPS
COOL. 13/05/1994

JASON LEONARD, ENGLAND. 01/06/1994

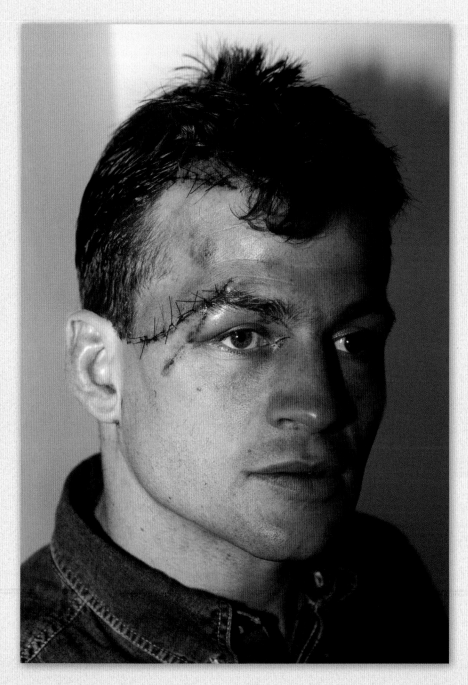

JON CALLARD, ENGLAND, SHOWS OFF
CUTS TO HIS HEAD. 07/06/1994

ENGLAND'S WILL GREENWOOD ON THE RECEIVING END OF A TACKLE. 06/12/1997

MARC DE ROUGEMONT, THE FRENCH HOOKER (C), PLAYING AGAINST SCOTLAND. 20/02/1998

ARWEL THOMAS OF WALES GOES TO GROUND. 21/02/1998

GARY PAGEL, NORTHAMPTON SAINTS (C). 23/02/1998

LEICESTER SCRUM HALF AUSTIN HEALEY. 13/02/1999

IRELAND'S KEITH WOOD (C) LEADS HIS PACK INTO A SCRUM AGAINST WALES. 20/02/1999

THE QUINNELL BROTHERS OF WALES, SCOTT (R) AND CRAIG (L) SING THE NATIONAL ANTHEM. 06/03/1999

ENGLAND'S FRONT ROW (L-R): DARREN GARFORTH, RICHARD COCKERILL, JASON LEONARD. 20/03/1999

CRAIG QUINNELL CELEBRATES A
WALES TRY. 11/04/1999

OPPOSITE

ENGLAND'S RICHARD HILL
CELEBRATES SCORING A TRY.
11/04/1999

WALES' CRAIG QUINNELL TELLS THE REFEREE TO KEEP HIS EYES OPEN. 23/10/1999

WASPS' ALEX KING TRIES TO ESCAPE FROM A SARACENS TACKLER. 07/11/1999

ENGLAND'S LAWRENCE DALLAGLIO (C) POWERS OVER FOR A TRY AS WALES' NEIL JENKINS (L) AND MARK TAYLOR (R)
ATTEMPT TO TACKLE HIM. 04/03/2000

ENGLAND CAPTAIN LAWRENCE DALLAGLIO (THIRD L) LEADS HIS TEAM IN SINGING THE NATIONAL ANTHEM.

18/03/2000

ROB HENDERSON CELEBRATES WITH STEVE BLACK AS THEY WALK OFF AT THE GABBA AFTER THE LIONS' VICTORY OVER AUSTRALIA IN THE FIRST TEST IN BRISBANE. 30/06/2001

OPPOSITE

IRELAND'S PAUL O'CONNELL CELEBRATES HIS TRY ON HIS TEST DEBUT AGAINST WALES. 03/02/2002

ENGLAND COACH SIR CLIVE WOODWARD DURING A PRESS CONFERENCE AT TWICKENHAM. 19/03/2004

WASPS' ALEX KING EVADES THE TACKLE OF TREVOR BRENNAN OF TOULOUSE TO SET UP WASPS' SECOND TRY DURING THE HEINEKEN CUP FINAL AT TWICKENHAM. 23/05/2004

A BLOODIED MARTIN JOHNSON,
LEICESTER CAPTAIN. 06/11/2004

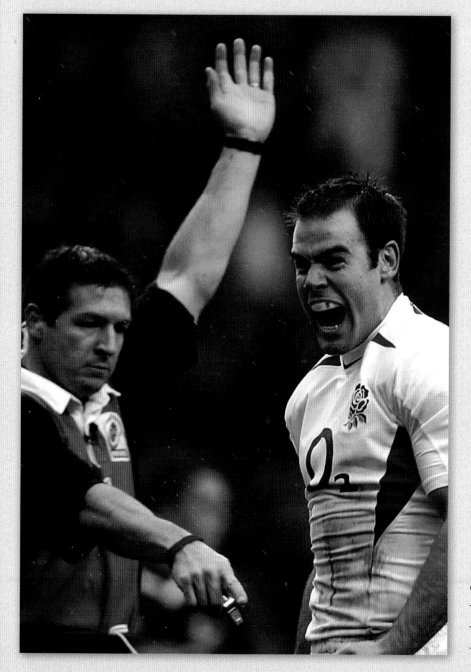

ENGLAND'S CHARLIE HODGSON
CELEBRATES SCORING THE OPENING
TRY AGAINST SOUTH AFRICA DURING
THE INTERNATIONAL MATCH AT
TWICKENHAM. 20/11/2004

WALES' KEVIN MORGAN (SECOND L) CELEBRATES HIS TRY WITH TEAMMATES STEPHEN JONES (L), SHANE WILLIAMS AND
GAVIN HENSON (R). 19/03/2005

OPPOSITE

BRITISH & IRISH LIONS' MICHAEL
OWEN. 11/06/2005

BRITISH & IRISH LIONS' JONNY WILKINSON. 24/06/2005

NEC HARLEQUINS' MEL DEANE IS
TACKLED BY LEICESTER TIGERS' OLLIE
SMITH. 23/09/2006

OSPREYS' JAMES HOOK CELEBRATES
AFTER A LAST MINUTE CONVERSION
DEFEATED SALE IN THE HEINEKEN
CUP MATCH AT THE LIBERTY
STADIUM, SWANSEA. 20/10/2006

SALE'S MAGNUS LUND WINS A LINE OUT AGAINST OSPREYS. 20/10/2006

LEICESTER'S MARTIN CORRY LOSES THE BALL AS HE IS TACKLED BY MUNSTER'S RONAN O'GARA. 22/10/2006

ENGLAND HEAD COACH ANDY ROBINSON DURING A PRESS CONFERENCE. 31/10/2006

WALES COACH GARETH JENKINS. 03/11/2006

NEW ZEALAND'S DAN CARTER IN ACTION AGAINST ENGLAND DURING THE INTERNATIONAL MATCH AT TWICKENHAM.
08/11/2006

ENGLAND CAPTAIN MARTIN CORRY FEEDS THE BALL OUT. 18/11/2006

ENGLAND COACH ANDY ROBINSON. 18/11/2006

GAVIN HENSON, OSPREYS. 15/12/2006

IAN MCGEECHAN, LONDON WASPS DIRECTOR OF RUGBY. 13/01/2007

SALE'S SEBASTIEN CHABAL PLEADS HIS INNOCENCE TO THE REFEREE AS HE RECEIVES A YELLOW CARD. 20/01/2007

SCOTLAND COACH FRANK HADDEN
POSES FOR A PICTURE DURING THE
LAUNCH OF THE RBS 6 NATIONS.
24/01/2007

WALES CAPTAIN STEPHEN JONES
DURING THE LAUNCH OF THE RBS 6
NATIONS. 24/01/2007

WALES' GARETH THOMAS DURING A TRAINING SESSION. 31/01/2007

MIKE TINDALL, ENGLAND. 03/02/2007

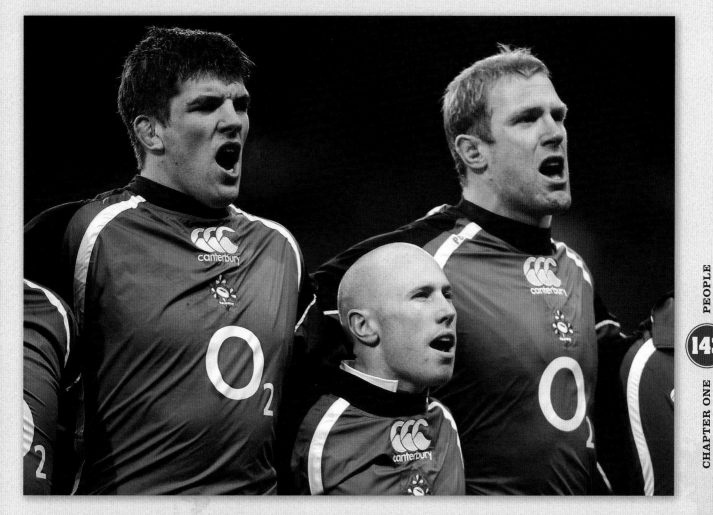

IRELAND'S DONNCHA O'CALLAGHAN (L), PETER STRINGER AND PAUL O'CONNELL SING THE NATIONAL ANTHEM BEFORE THE RBS 6 NATIONS MATCH AGAINST ENGLAND AT CROKE PARK, DUBLIN. 24/02/2007

WALES' SHANE WILLIAMS CELEBRATES. 10/03/2007

ENGLAND'S JULIEN WHITE (L) AND FRANCE'S OLIVIER MILLOUD (R) FACE EACH OTHER IN THE SCRUM. 11/03/2007

ENGLAND'S MIKE CATT KICKS THE BALL DOWN FIELD. 17/03/2007

OPPOSITE

LEICESTER'S TOM VARNDELL (C) SENDS A PASS OUT. 21/04/2007

LONDON WASPS' LAWRENCE DALLAGLIO (L) SPEAKS TO NORTHAMPTON SAINTS' CARLOS SPENCER (R). 22/04/2007

LEICESTER TIGERS' MARTIN CORRY WINS A LINE OUT. 12/05/2007

ENGLAND'S ANDY FARRELL DURING AN IRB RUGBY WORLD CUP MATCH AGAINST THE USA. 08/09/2007

ENGLAND'S JONNY WILKINSON DURING KICKING PRACTICE. 27/09/2007

ENGLAND'S PAUL SACKEY SCORES HIS SECOND TRY OF THE MATCH AGAINST TONGA. 28/09/2007

ENGLAND'S JONNY WILKINSON LOOKS ON AT THE SCRUM. 13/10/2007

Chapter Two
PLACES

GREAT GROUNDS

The famous stadiums are where dreams are made and broken

They call it the Cabbage Patch, because that's what it once was. Look at early photos of Twickenham Stadium, home of the Rugby Football Union, and you can see its origins, its cabbage roots. Photos from the 1920s show it surrounded by fields, a former market garden a long way from the London city that has since grown to embrace it. Even then, a huge car park was needed, and when the stadium was first built they also had to build roads so that people could actually get there.

From these simple beginnings, Twickenham has grown into the largest rugby stadium in Britain, capable of holding 82,000 people. Indeed, only the new Wembley Stadium is bigger. But when Twickenham was first built, it was designed to hold just 20,000 spectators.

Work began on the ground in 1907, when the Rugby Football Union decided it would be a good idea to

own their own stadium. People wanted to see visiting teams like South Africa and New Zealand. England's first ever home match against New Zealand (England lost 15-0) was held at Crystal Palace in 1905.

So it was the Rugby Football Union invested £5,572 and loose change to acquire about 10 acres of market garden in leafy Twickenham, built their roads and their stands, and Twickenham Stadium was open for business when Harlequins played Richmond on 2 October 1909, followed by its first international, when England beat Wales 11-6.

It would be 23 years before Wales would win at Twickenham, an indication of why places and stadiums are important in the game. They become characters in the story, they turn into symbols and good-luck charms, sources of national pride and arenas of combat where great dramas are played out.

SCOTLAND'S GROUNDS

In 1897 Scotland had become the first of the home Rugby Unions to own its own ground when it bought land at Inverleath and constructed the world's first purpose-built rugby stadium there. It didn't last very long, however, as during the First World War it was rather neglected and then after the war there was a boom in rugby attendances, and poor old Inverleath couldn't cope. A new ground was needed.

The new ground was found at Murrayfield, and on 21 March 1925 England became the first international team to play there, losing 14-11 to give Scotland their first-ever Five Nations Grand Slam. Murrayfield was a stadium worthy of a winning team, and though its capacity today is a fairly

ABOVE
VIEW OF MURRAYFIELD.
03/02/1996

OPPOSITE
VIEW OF TWICKENHAM.
03/01/1925

modest 67,800, it holds the world record attendance figure for a Rugby Union match, when 104,000 people watched Scotland play Wales on 1 March 1975.

It's unlikely that such numbers will be seen again with today's trend for more compact all-seater stadiums. The generations of fans who have attended such matches, when all-standing was the way most people watched a match, will know that something has disappeared from the game.

GROUNDS IN WALES

That's not to say that today's stadiums don't have characters of their own, as anyone who has visited Cardiff's stunning Millennium Stadium will understand. It stands right in the heart of the city, just as rugby is right at the heart of the Welsh nation. That stadium was permeated by passion and history before it was even opened, in 1999.

It stands alongside the previous home of Welsh rugby, the famous Cardiff Arms Park, the very name of which still brings pride to Welsh fans and a little trepidation to everyone else. The original Cardiff Arms was a pub across the road, where players changed before matches. The area had been a swampy and not very desirable part of the city when the Victorian engineer Isambard Kingdom Brunel diverted

CARDIFF ARMS PARK DURING A MATCH. 12/03/1932

the River Taff to enable him to bring the railway to Cardiff, and this had the effect of also draining the swamp. By 1882 a small 300-seater stand had been built and gradually the ground emerged from the swamps, though occasionally the swamp would re-emerge from the ground, as some of the early photographs show. In fact the state of the pitch was a common cause for complaint, and eventually work on a brand new National Stadium began in 1970 although it wasn't to be completed for a further 14 years. And then, only 13 years after that, it was considered too small and was demolished to make way for the Millennium Stadium.

On 26 June 1999 Wales christened the stadium by beating South Africa 29-19 in a friendly match setting the way for the 1999 Rugby World Cup, held mainly in Wales later that year. Unfortunately Wales lost 24-9 to Australia in the tournament's quarter-finals, also at the Millennium Stadium. With its sliding roof and grass that can be taken up and replaced to enable non-sporting events to be held there, the Millennium Stadium is indeed a ground that's ready for rugby's next 100 years.

AUSTRALIA'S CHRIS LATHAM CELEBRATES HIS FIRST TRY AGAINST WALES DURING THE INTERNATIONAL MATCH AT THE MILLENNIUM STADIUM, CARDIFF. 04/11/2006

THE TWO CAPTAINS ARE INTRODUCED TO KING GEORGE V BEFORE THE MATCH.

OXFORD UNIVERSITY V CAMBRIDGE UNIVERSITY, QUEEN'S CLUB. 07/12/1919

VIEW OF TWICKENHAM BEFORE THE MATCH BETWEEN ENGLAND AND NEW ZEALAND. 03/01/1925

AERIAL VIEW OF TWICKENHAM. 01/06/1928

THE TWO TEAMS LINE UP BEFORE THE MATCH AS THE BRASS BAND PLAYS. VARSITY MATCH, OXFORD UNIVERSITY V CAMBRIDGE UNIVERSITY, TWICKENHAM. 11/12/1928

BRISTOL CAPTAIN F.W. TUCKER (L) LEADS HIS TEAM OUT AT TWICKENHAM. 05/11/1938

OPPOSITE

AERIAL VIEW OF TWICKENHAM. 01/06/1932

WALES' LES WILLIAMS (C) KICKS DOWNFIELD AT CARDIFF ARMS PARK. 18/01/1947

WORKMEN IN THE PROCESS OF INSTALLING THE NEW TWICKENHAM WEATHER VANE, DESIGNED BY KENNETH DALGLIESH, WHICH FEATURES HERMES, THE MESSENGER OF THE GODS, PASSING A BALL TO A MODERN-DAY RUGBY PLAYER.

18/01/1950

THE NEW ZEALAND SQUAD TRAINING AT EASTBOURNE COLLEGE. 23/10/1953

OPPOSITE

WALES CAPTAIN LEWIS JONES IS CARRIED SHOULDER HIGH BY JUBILANT WELSH
FANS WHO SPILLED ONTO THE TWICKENHAM PITCH AT THE FINAL WHISTLE.
21/01/1950

A SIGN OUTSIDE TWICKENHAM PROHIBITING PHOTOGRAPHY INSIDE THE GROUND. 23/02/1957

THE TWICKENHAM CROWD OBSERVES A MINUTE'S SILENCE IN MEMORY OF THE MANCHESTER UNITED PLAYERS KILLED IN THE MUNICH AIR DISASTER TWO DAYS BEFORE. 08/02/1958

FRANCE'S ANTOINE LABAZUY (10) KICKS A PENALTY TO SCORE FRANCE'S ONLY POINTS IN A 3-3 TIE WITH ENGLAND AT TWICKENHAM. 28/02/1959

VIEW OF THE ACTION AT TWICKENHAM AS FRANCE'S JEAN-VINCENT DUPUY KICKS FOR TOUCH TO RELIEVE ENGLISH
PRESSURE. 28/02/1959

FRANCE FANS SPRAY CHAMPAGNE ON THEIR COCKEREL MASCOT ON THE TWICKENHAM PITCH BEFORE THE GAME AGAINST ENGLAND. 28/02/1959

IRELAND'S TONY O'REILLY (THIRD L) HOLDS ONTO THE BALL AS HE IS FORCED INTO TOUCH WHILE PLAYING WALES AT CARDIFF ARMS PARK. 14/03/1959

IRELAND'S SYD MILLAR (C) CLAIMS THE BALL AT LANSDOWNE ROAD. 17/12/1960

OPPOSITE

ACTION AT MURRAYFIELD. 11/02/1961

GENERAL VIEW OF ACTION FROM THE MATCH. OTAGO V BRITISH LIONS, CARISBROOK. 05/06/1993

OPPOSITE

THE CROWD STREAMS ONTO THE TWICKENHAM PITCH. 28/02/1970

A LINE OUT UNDER TWICKENHAM'S NEW FLOODLIGHTS. 12/12/1995

THE FIJI RUGBY TEAM TRAINING AT OXFORD UNIVERSITY. 11/11/1998

ACTION FROM THE 'A' INTERNATIONAL PLAYED AT REDRUTH RFC GROUND. ENGLAND 'A' V FRANCE 'A'. 19/03/1999

WALES CAPTAIN ROB HOWLEY (C) LEADS OUT THE WELSH TEAM FOR THE FIRST EVER MATCH IN THE MILLENNIUM STADIUM, AGAINST SOUTH AFRICA. 26/06/1999

A GLORIOUS RAINBOW GREETS ENGLAND AND ITALY AS THEY EMERGE FOR THE SECOND HALF OF THEIR RUGBY WORLD CUP GROUP B GAME AT TWICKENHAM. 02/10/1999

THE MILLENNIUM STADIUM PRESS BOX. 23/10/1999

THE WELSH CROWD AT THE MILLENNIUM STADIUM, CARDIFF SHOW THEIR SUPPORT FOR THE WALES TEAM AFTER THEY ARE KNOCKED OUT OF THE WORLD CUP BY AUSTRALIA. 23/10/1999

THE BRITISH LIONS SQUAD WARM UP IN BRISBANE FOR THEIR GAME WITH QUEENSLAND REDS.19/06/2001

WALES' MARK JONES DURING TRAINING AT THE CANBERRA RAIDERS TRAINING FIELDS. 21/10/2003

OPPOSITE

ENGLAND'S SQUAD DURING A TRAINING SESSION AT THE PENNYHILL PARK

HOTEL IN BAGSHOT, SURREY. 20/11/2002

FOG DECENDS IN THE WASPS AND LLANELLI CONTEST DURING THE HEINEKEN CUP MATCH AT STRADEY PARK. 11/12/2005

A LONDON WASPS PLAYER KICKING AT TWICKENHAM. 02/09/2006

LEICESTER TIGERS AND LONDON WASPS PLAYERS IN A SCRUM DURING THE GUINNESS PREMIERSHIP MATCH AT ADAMS PARK, WYCOMBE. 26/11/2006

LEICESTER TIGERS AND LONDON
WASPS PLAYERS REGROUP AFTER
THEIR SCRUMS KEEP COLLAPSING
DURING THE GUINNESS PREMIERSHIP
MATCH AT ADAMS PARK, WYCOMBE.
26/11/2006

LEICESTER AND BRISTOL PACKS CREATE A HEAD OF STEAM DURING THE GUINNESS PREMIERSHIP MATCH AT WELFORD ROAD, LEICESTER. 22/12/2006

WASPS' TOM PALMER WINS A LINE OUT AGAINST BATH DURING THE GUINNESS PREMIERSHIP MATCH AT THE RECREATION GROUND, BATH. 01/01/2007

THE PITCH AT THE MEMORIAL STADIUM, BRISTOL. 07/01/2007

OPPOSITE

TWICKENHAM PRIOR TO THE

HEINEKEN CUP FINAL. 20/05/2007

SCOTLAND PLAYERS DURING A
TRAINING SESSION ON THE BACK
PITCHES AT MURRAYFIELD,
EDINBURGH. 20/08/2007

WALES' ALUN-WYN JONES AND FRANCE'S FABIEN PELOUS COMPETE FOR A LINE OUT DURING THE INVESCO PERPETUAL SUMMER SERIES MATCH AT THE MILLENNIUM STADIUM, CARDIFF. 26/08/2007

ENGLAND'S JONNY WILKINSON LANDS HIS FOURTH AND THE WINNING PENALTY AGAINST AUSTRALIA DURING THE IRB RUGBY WORLD CUP QUARTER FINAL MATCH AT STADE VELODROME, MARSEILLE, FRANCE. 06/10/2007

THE CROWD HAVE TO SHIELD THEIR EYES FROM THE LATE AFTERNOON SUN. BRISTOL RUGBY V LLANELLI SCARLETS, THE MEMORIAL STADIUM. 28/10/2007

Chapter Three
MOMENTS

HIGHS AND LOWS

One man's triumph is another man's disaster

But when the triumphs come, how we like to savour them, fan and player alike. Everyone who watched the World Cup Final in 2003 will remember the ending down the years, as no fiction writer could have dared produce such a dramatic climax. When Jonny Wilkinson hit that drop-goal to produce a last-gasp win for England with just seconds on the clock, he was reminding us what sport is all about: skill and drama combined.

WORLD CUP 1995

It wasn't the first time England had triumphed with such a late and breathtaking drop-goal, the score which in some ways is cleaner and purer than a try, the perfect pivotal moment when a game swings and hands victory to a team with one action. It had happened back in 1995, too, also in the World Cup.

And as if some invisible deity were writing the script, developing the plot towards that 2003 moment, the opponents were England and Australia again. It was the quarter-final this time, the reward a place in the semifinal against New Zealand or Scotland, who were playing later in the afternoon. The scores were tied and the hero this day was Rob Andrew, whose last-minute drop, showing grace under pressure, sent England through.

Those moments are rare and fleeting, though, which is why we cherish them so much. But triumphs and disasters are not just about last-minute wins, they flow like blood through the body of the game. Some last a moment, others last a tournament, and some last a lifetime.

WORLD CUP 2007

It was a disaster for England when Jason Robinson limped off the field early in the 2007 World Cup, and seemingly out of the game forever, in a pool match against South Africa. One of rugby's recent great talents, he had been coaxed out of retirement to

OPPOSITE
A SILVERSMITH MAKES THE
NECESSARY MODIFICATIONS TO
ADD THE ITALIAN EMBLEM TO
THE SIX NATIONS TROPHY
(FORMERLY FIVE NATIONS).
13/01/2000

LEFT
ENGLAND CAPTAIN MARTIN
JOHNSON CELEBRATES WITH
THE WEBB ELLIS TROPHY.
22/11/2003

show his skills again. But the misfortune of a sudden injury, one of those other moments that can turn matches, seemed to have brought a sad end to a glorious career. Fate hadn't finished with us yet, though, as Robinson recovered, and led the team out as captain in his 50th game, which just happened to be a semi-final against the host nation, France. Robinson and his team triumphed, only for him to leave the field again in the final, injured in a game that saw South Africa lift the trophy.

THE RBS 6 NATIONS
Here in Britain we have the excitement of the RBS 6 Nations every year, the ebb and flow of success and failure. Despite being played by the same teams at the same time every year, in the simplest of contests, it seems without fail to produce thrills and great tries, and all the drama of a Shakespeare play, albeit one that lasts several weeks.

The whole production goes back to 1883, when the four home nations of England, Scotland, Ireland and Wales decided to mount a tournament. They had been playing each other off and on in friendly matches ever since a Scotland-England encounter in 1871, which is generally regarded as the first international match. It was a simple formula from the start, with each team playing each other team once, but in that very simplicity lies its success. All great drama has a simple formula.

England won that first series, and in the process invented the notion of the Triple Crown, by beating the other three nations. An extra layer had been added, to be enhanced yet again when France officially joined the tournament in 1910 and the Four Nations became the Five Nations. Beat all four other teams and you claim the triumph of the Grand Slam (Wales did it first, in 1911).

With the dawn of the new century in 2000, Italy joined the fray and the RBS 6 Nations was created.

THE MIDDLESEX SEVENS

Another hallowed tournament that has seen its share of triumphs and disasters is the Middlesex Sevens,

ABOVE

ENGLAND'S JONNY WILKINSON KICKS THE WINNING DROP GOAL TO CLINCH THE RUGBY WORLD CUP FOR ENGLAND IN THE FINAL SECONDS OF A THRILLING FINAL BETWEEN AUSTRALIA AND ENGLAND. 22/11/2003

OPPOSITE ABOVE

LONDON WASPS CAPTAIN LAWRENCE DALLAGLIO AND DIRECTOR OF RUGBY IAN MCGEECHAN CELEBRATE WITH THE HEINEKEN CUP. 20/05/2007

that scaled-down version of the game that has been held at Twickenham every summer since 1926, even during the World War Two years. It was a showcase for the skills of players like Wavell Wakefield, the captain of Harlequins, who won the Sevens for the first four years of its life. The Harlequins have been one of the dominant teams in the knockout tournament, along with London Welsh and Richmond, while in recent years Rugby League teams were invited to compete in this event. Two of them – Wigan in 1996 and Bradford Bulls in 2002 – won.

OTHER TOURNAMENTS

In 1987 the Guinness Premiership was introduced, to provide week in week out competition for the top English club teams, while other tournaments have provided other dramas. In 1995 the Heineken Cup was launched, allowing British and Irish fans a chance to see great club teams like Toulouse and Perpignan play. In 2001 the Celtic League (now the Magners League) allowed regional teams from Scotland, Wales and Ireland to compete against each other, with the Celtic Cup arriving in 2003. The Anglo-Welsh Cup (now the EDF Energy Anglo-Welsh Cup) lets English and Welsh teams compete against each other too.

No matter what the competition, or how they change as one becomes another or changes its name, rugby remains a game of team against team, each seeking to triumph, or to avoid disaster. And from all those games occasional gems emerge to remind us what rugby is all about. Skill and drama. Grace under pressure. Triumph and disaster.

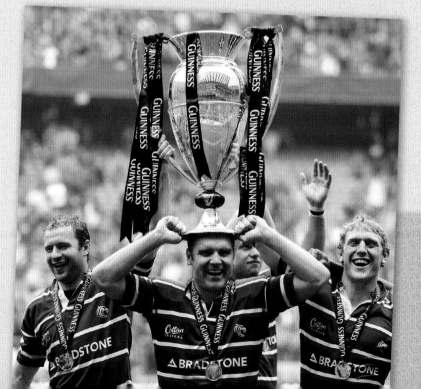

LEFT
LEICESTER TIGERS' ANDY GOODE CELEBRATES WITH THE CUP AT THE GUINNESS PREMIERSHIP FINAL MATCH. 12/05/2007

A LINE OUT BETWEEN ENGLAND AND SCOTLAND AT THE BRITISH AND IRISH CHAMPIONSHIP. 09/03/1901

SCOTLAND'S JOHN DALLAS (R) TOUCHES DOWN TO SCORE A TRY AGAINST ENGLAND. 21/03/1903

CAMBRIDGE UNIVERSITY ON THE ATTACK DURING THE VARSITY MATCH AGAINST OXFORD UNIVERSITY. 07/12/1919

THE DUKE OF YORK SHAKES HANDS WITH THE ENGLAND PLAYERS BEFORE THE MATCH IN THE FIVE NATIONS
CHAMPIONSHIP AGAINST IRELAND. 11/02/1933

ST MARY'S HOSPITAL DEFEATED KING'S COLLEGE HOSPITAL BY 11 POINTS TO 3 IN THE FINAL OF THE HOSPITAL RUGBY CUP
AT RICHMOND ATHLETIC GROUND. PHOTO SHOWS W.E. HENLEY, CAPTAIN OF ST MARY'S HOSPITAL, WITH THE CUP, BEING
CHEERED BY MEMBERS OF THE TEAM. 20/03/1935

THE AUSTRALIAN RUGBY TEAM ARRIVE IN ENGLAND FOR THEIR TOUR OF BRITAIN. (L-R) BILL MCLEAN (CAPTAIN), ARNOLD TANCRED (MANAGER), TREVOR ALLAN (VICE CAPTAIN) AND MASCOT 'WALLY'. 25/08/1947

THE IRELAND PLAYERS ARE MOBBED BY JUBILANT FANS AT THE FINAL WHISTLE, AFTER THEY HELD OFF ENGLAND 11-10.

14/02/1948

WALES' JACK MATTHEWS (R) TOUCHES DOWN FOR A TRY IN THE FIVE NATIONS CHAMPIONSHIP AGAINST FRANCE.
25/03/1950

THE TRIUMPHANT LONDON WELSH TEAM, WITH CAPTAIN CARWYN JAMES (C) HOLDING THE RUSSELL-CARGILL MEMORIAL CUP. 24/04/1956

OPPOSITE

WALES' KEN JONES (L) TOUCHES DOWN TO SCORE A TRY BEFORE ENGLAND'S WILLIAM HOOK (R) CAN TACKLE HIM DURING THE FIVE NATIONS CHAMPIONSHIP. 19/01/1952

ENGLAND'S PETER THOMPSON (C) DIVES OVER TO SCORE HIS TEAM'S SECOND TRY IN THE FIVE NATIONS CHAMPIONSHIP MATCH AGAINST SCOTLAND. 16/03/1957

SOUTH AFRICA'S HANNES BREWIS (R) KICKS TO TOUCH AS WALES' REES STEPHENS (L) GIVES CHASE DURING A TOUR MATCH. 23/12/1957

IRELAND'S JACKIE KYLE (C) IS CHAIRED OFF THE PITCH BY HIS TEAMMATES AFTER THE FIVE NATIONS CHAMPIONSHIP
MATCH AGAINST ENGLAND, HIS 45TH CAP. 08/02/1958

FRANCE'S LUCIEN MIAS (C) GRABS A LOOSE BALL DURING THE FIVE NATIONS CHAMPIONSHIP MATCH AGAINST WALES.
29/03/1958

LEICESTER'S HERBERT 'CHALKIE' WHITE RELEASES THE BALL TO HIS BACKS. HARLEQUINS V LEICESTER AT TWICKENHAM.
27/09/1958

WALES' BRYN MEREDITH (THIRD R) LOSES THE BALL AS HE IS TACKLED DURING THE FIVE NATIONS CHAMPIONSHIP MATCH AGAINST ENGLAND. 17/01/1959

ENGLAND'S DICKIE JEEPS (L) STOOPS TO GATHER THE BALL AS HIS TEAMMATES HOLD BACK THE WALES PLAYERS IN A LOOSE MAUL. 16/01/1960

OPPOSITE

ENGLAND'S RICHARD SHARP (C) KICKS DOWNFIELD AFTER BEATING A TACKLE BY FRANCE'S PIERRE LACROIX (R). 23/02/1963

TWO WESTFIELD COLLEGE PLAYERS
LEAVE THE PITCH AFTER THE MATCH,
PLAYED AFTER ONE OF THE GIRLS
CHALLENGED A MALE POST-
GRADUATE TO A GAME. 18/03/1963

PUPILS FROM ST GEORGE'S COLLEGE, WEYBRIDGE, WATCH THE ENGLAND TEAM TRAINING ON THEIR SCHOOL FIELDS.
07/02/1964

BARBARIANS' IAN CLARKE TACKLES NEW ZEALAND'S COLIN MEADS AT CARDIFF ARMS PARK. 15/02/1964

WALES CAPTAIN CLIVE ROWLANDS IS CHAIRED FROM THE PITCH BY JUBILANT SUPPORTERS AFTER HIS TEAM WRAPPED UP
THE TRIPLE CROWN WITH VICTORY OVER IRELAND. 13/03/1965

AUSTRALIA SCRUM HALF KEN CATCHPOLE FEEDS HIS BACKS WHILE PLAYING AGAINST ENGLAND. 07/01/1967

NEW ZEALAND CAPTAIN BRIAN LOCHORE IS CHAIRED OFF BY HIS TRIUMPHANT TEAMMATES AFTER LEADING HIS TEAM TO VICTORY IN THE FINAL GAME OF THE TOUR OF BRITAIN. THE GAME WAS AGAINST BARBARIANS. 16/12/1967

THE BALL SAILS BETWEEN THE POSTS AS FRANCE'S GUY CAMBERABERO CONVERTS HIS TEAM'S SECOND TRY AGAINST WALES. 23/03/1968

OPPOSITE

NEW ZEALAND CAPTAIN BRIAN LOCHORE (L) LEADS HIS TEAMMATES IN A FAREWELL HAKA BEFORE BOARDING THE PLANE HOME AFTER THEIR TOUR OF BRITAIN. 18/12/1967

FRANCE CAPTAIN CHRISTIAN CARRERE
IS CHAIRED OFF THE PITCH BY HIS
JUBILANT TEAMMATES AFTER THEIR
14-9 WIN SECURED FRANCE'S FIRST
FIVE NATIONS GRAND SLAM.
23/03/1968

(L-R) WALES' MAURICE RICHARDS GETS AWAY FROM IRELAND'S ALAN DUGGAN DURING THE MATCH IN THE FIVE NATIONS CHAMPIONSHIP. 08/03/1969

TWO ANTI-APARTHEID DEMONSTRATORS WHO CLIMBED TO THE TOP OF THE GOALPOSTS DURING THE SPRINGBOKS
MATCH AT ABERDEEN. 02/12/1969

OPPOSITE

AN ANTI-APARTHEID DEMONSTRATOR IS ESCORTED OFF THE TWICKENHAM
PITCH DURING THE SPRINGBOKS TOUR OF THE UK. 05/11/1969

WALES' BARRY JOHN (R) TOUCHES DOWN TO SCORE A TRY AGAINST ENGLAND DURING THE FIVE NATIONS CHAMPIONSHIP. 28/02/1970

FRANCE'S PIERRE VILLEPREUX CONVERTS A TRY AGAINST ENGLAND DURING THE FIVE NATIONS CHAMPIONSHIP.

27/02/1971

WALES' JOHN TAYLOR IS CARRIED OFF BY THE CROWD AFTER HIS TEAM'S 35-12 VICTORY AGAINST SCOTLAND. 05/02/1972

JOHN WILLIAMS, SAFELY OVER THE LINE FOR THE BARBARIANS' LAST TRY AGAINST NEW ZEALAND AT CARDIFF ARMS PARK.
27/01/1973

A MALE STREAKER COVERED BY A
COAT IS LED AWAY BY POLICE AFTER
RACING ACROSS THE FIELD IN FRONT
OF 45,000 SPECTATORS, AT HALF TIME
DURING THE CHARITY SPECIAL
INTERNATIONAL BETWEEN ENGLAND
AND FRANCE AT TWICKENHAM.
20/04/1974

ENGLAND'S MIKE BURTON CHANGES
HIS SHORTS DURING THE FIVE
NATIONS CHAMPIONSHIP MATCH
AGAINST SCOTLAND. 15/03/1975

ST MARYS' P. RAWLE MAKES HIS WAY TO THE TRY LINE THROUGH THE TACKLES AND THE BLIZZARD DURING THE HOSPITALS CUP AGAINST WESTMINSTER. 09/02/1978

WALES' GARETH EDWARDS (C) FAKES A PASS TO THE WING, DECEIVING SCOTLAND'S ALASTAIR CRANSTON (L). 18/02/1978

FRANCE'S JEAN-PIERRE BASTIAT (THIRD L) WINS THE LINE OUT BALL AHEAD OF WALES' DEREK QUINNELL (THIRD R) DURING THE FIVE NATIONS CHAMPIONSHIP. 18/03/1978

A LINE OUT BATTLE DURING THE FIVE NATIONS MATCH BETWEEN WALES AND FRANCE AT CARDIFF ARMS PARK. WALES WON THE MATCH 16-7 TO TAKE THE CHAMPIONSHIP GRAND SLAM. 18/03/1978

WALES' PHIL BENNETT (SECOND L) TOUCHES DOWN HIS TEAM'S FIRST TRY DESPITE THE EFFORTS OF FRANCE'S JEAN-MICHEL AGUIRRE (L) AND JEROME GALLION (THIRD L), AS THE WELSH TEAM MARCH ON TO THE GRAND SLAM. 18/03/1978

(L-R) TONY WARD, IRISH FLY-HALF; GARETH EDWARDS, WELSH RETIRED PLAYER; AND SCOTTISH ATTACKER ANDY IRVINE, PROUDLY SHOW OFF THEIR 'GOLDEN BOOT' AWARDS PRESENTED AT PAINTERS' HALL IN LONDON. 28/09/1978

FORMER WELSH PLAYER GARETH
EDWARDS PROUDLY SHOWS OFF HIS
'GOLDEN BOOT' AWARD, WHICH HE
RECEIVED AT A CEREMONY IN
PAINTERS' HALL IN LONDON.
28/09/1978

THE ENGLAND V SCOTLAND CALCUTTA CUP MATCH AT TWICKENHAM ENDED WITH A 7-7 DRAW. IN THIS PICTURE, COMING OUT OF THE SCRUM (L-R), ENGLAND'S M.RAFTER, R.M.UTLEY (CAPTAIN), M.YOUNG (BALL), REFEREE C.NORLING, AND SCOTLAND'S CAPTAIN I.R.MCGEECHAN. 03/02/1979

LANCASHIRE'S BILL BEAUMONT (C) LAYS THE BALL BACK TO A TEAMMATE DURING THE COUNTY CHAMPIONSHIP SEMI FINAL AGAINST SURREY. 08/12/1979

THE ENGLAND RUGBY TEAM, AT THE DORCHESTER HOTEL IN LONDON AFTER THEY RECEIVED THE RUGBY UNION TEAM OF THE YEAR TROPHY 1980, HELD BY THEIR CAPTAIN, BILL BEAUMONT. 17/04/1980

LEICESTER'S PETER WHEELER (L) AND ROBIN COWLING (R) HOLD UP THE JOHN PLAYER CUP. 02/05/1981

OPPOSITE

THE ENGLAND RUGBY TEAM GAVE BRITAIN A LIFT AS THEY GOT TOGETHER TO
RAISE UP THIS MINI METRO WITH UNION JACK PAINTWORK, WHILST TRAINING
FOR THEIR UPCOMING MATCH AGAINST FRANCE. 19/03/1981

ENGLAND'S PETER WHEELER (FOURTH L) HELPS TO KEEP THE SCOTLAND FORWARDS AT BAY AS TEAMMATE STEPHEN BOYLE (THIRD L) FEEDS SCRUM HALF STEVE SMITH (SECOND L) DURING THE FIVE NATIONS CHAMPIONSHIP MATCH. 05/03/1983

GLOUCESTERSHIRE CAPTAIN MIKE RAFTER HOLDS ALOFT THE TROPHY AT TWICKENHAM AFTER LEADING HIS TEAM TO 36-18 VICTORY OVER SOMERSET IN THE THORN EMI COUNTY CHAMPIONSHIP. 01/04/1984

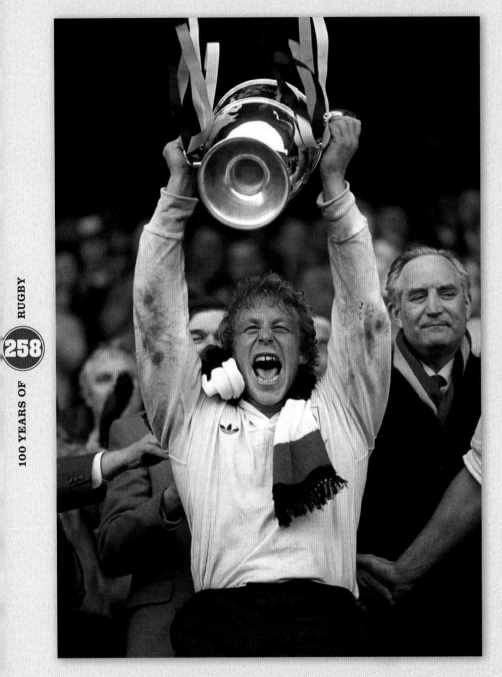

BATH CAPTAIN ROGER SPURRELL
HOLDS ALOFT THE JOHN PLAYER
SPECIAL CUP, WHICH HIS SIDE
RETAINED WHEN THEY BEAT LONDON
WELSH 24-15. 27/04/1985

SCOTLAND CAPTAIN DAVID SOLE (C) LEADING HIS TEAM IN CELEBRATION AFTER THEIR GRAND SLAM FIVE NATIONS RUGBY
CHAMPIONSHIP VICTORY OVER ENGLAND AT MURRAYFIELD. 17/03/1990

ENGLAND'S MIKE TEAGUE (C) PASSES THE BALL BACK TO RICHARD HILL (L) IN THE WORLD CUP SEMI FINAL AGAINST SCOTLAND. ENGLAND WON THIS MATCH ONLY TO BE BEATEN 12-6 BY AUSTRALIA IN THE FINAL. 26/10/1991

ENGLAND'S DEAN RICHARDS, DEWI MORRIS AND MARTIN BAYFIELD CARRIED BY FANS AFTER WINNING THE GRAND SLAM.
07/03/1992

THE BRITISH & IRISH LIONS LOOK ON AS THE NEW ZEALAND MAORIS PERFORM THE HAKA. 29/05/1993

ACTION AT A LINE OUT. FIVE NATIONS MATCH, ENGLAND V IRELAND. 19/02/1994

(L-R) ENGLAND'S MIKE CATT, KYRAN BRACKEN, NEIL BACK AND RICHARD WEST BALANCE ON SURF BOARDS ON THE BEACH IN DURBAN, SOUTH AFRICA. 25/05/1995

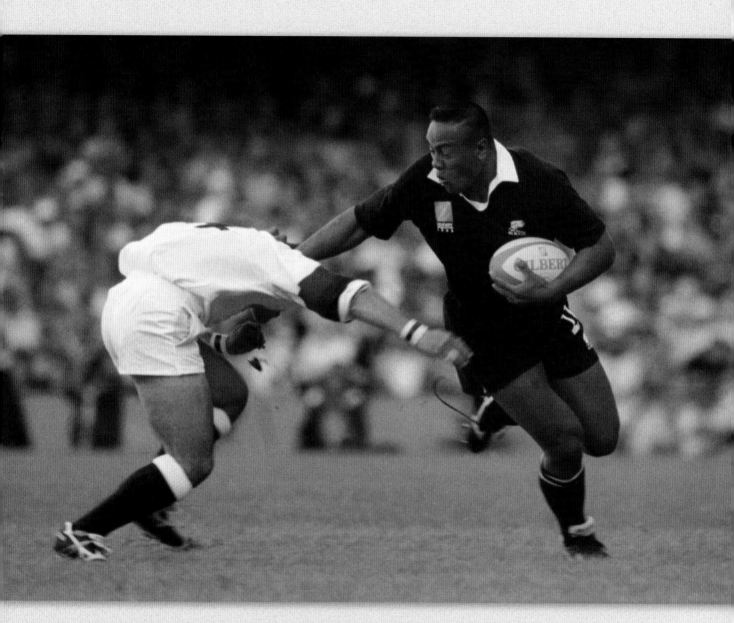

ENGLAND'S TONY UNDERWOOD TRIES TO TACKLE NEW ZEALAND'S JONAH LOMU. 18/06/1995

WILL CARLING OF ENGLAND LOOKS
DEJECTED AS THEY FALL FURTHER
BEHIND DURING THE RUGBY WORLD
CUP SEMI FINAL AGAINST NEW
ZEALAND. 18/06/1995

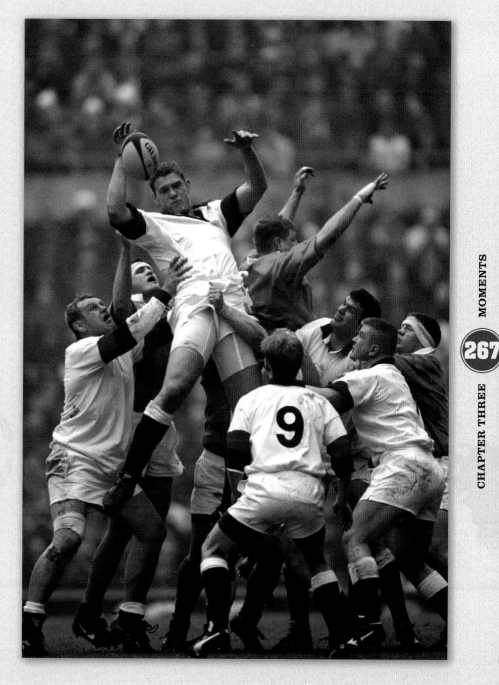

GARATH ARCHER OF ENGLAND JUMPS
FOR THE BALL IN A LINE OUT
AGAINST IRELAND. 16/03/1996

LAWRENCE DALLAGLIO SCORES A TRY FOR ENGLAND AS FRANCE'S PHILIPPE CARBONNEAU ATTEMPTS A TACKLE.

01/03/1997

JEREMY GUSCOTT CELEBRATES AT THE END OF THE GAME AFTER A LIONS VICTORY. 28/06/1997

THE ENGLAND TEAM STAND ARM IN
ARM BEFORE THE MATCH AGAINST
WALES. 21/02/1998

SARACENS' FRANCOIS PIENAAR AND MICHAEL LYNAGH LIFT THE TETLEY'S BITTER CUP. 09/05/1998

LLANELLI'S RUPERT MOON CELEBRATES VICTORY WITH HUGH WILLIAMS-JONES IN THE SWALEC CUP FINAL. 23/05/1998

RUPERT MOON, LLANELLI, CELEBRATES WITH SUPPORTERS AT THE SWALEC CUP FINAL. 23/05/1998

ENGLAND'S DAN LUGER CELEBRATES HIS TRY FOR ENGLAND AGAINST SCOTLAND. 20/02/1999

OPPOSITE

NICK BEAL OF ENGLAND TRIES TO MARK A HIGH BALL IN A FIVE NATIONS

CHAMPIONSHIP GAME AGAINST SCOTLAND. 20/02/1999

LEICESTER PLAYER AUSTIN HEALEY CELEBRATES HIS LAST MINUTE WINNING TRY AS TEAMMATE GEORDAN MURPHY (R) LOOKS ON, ON THE OPENING DAY OF THE SEASON, IN THEIR ZURICH PREMIERSHIP MATCH AGAINST WASPS AT LOFTUS ROAD, LONDON. 19/08/2000

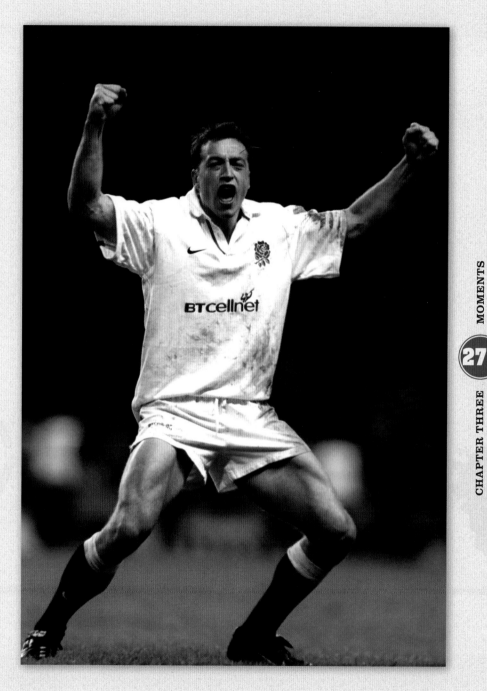

ENGLAND'S DAN LUGER CELEBRATES
SCORING THE WINNING TRY IN THE
LAST MINUTE IN A FRIENDLY AGAINST
AUSTRALIA. 18/11/2000

ENGLAND'S WILL GREENWOOD CELEBRATES SCORING THE OPENING TRY OF THE GAME AGAINST SOUTH AFRICA.

02/12/2000

BRITISH AND IRISH LIONS' ROB HENDERSON (L) AND KEITH WOOD LOOK DEJECTED AFTER LOSING THE THIRD TEST
MATCH AGAINST AUSTRALIA AT STADIUM AUSTRALIA, SYDNEY. 14/07/2001

LONDON IRISH'S CHRIS SHEASBY CELEBRATES WITH THE POWERGEN CUP AFTER THEIR VICTORY OVER NORTHAMPTON.
20/04/2002

GLOUCESTER CELEBRATE AFTER WINNING THE ZURICH CHAMPIONSHIP FINAL AT TWICKENHAM. 08/06/2002

NORTHAMPTON'S STEVE THOMPSON GOES OVER THE TOP OF BATH'S DANNY GREWCOCK (R) AND GARETH COOPER DURING SAINTS' 30-29 VICTORY IN THE POWERGEN QUARTER FINAL MATCH. 25/01/2003

THE ENGLAND TEAM CELEBRATE THEIR GRAND SLAM IN THE RBS 6 NATIONS CHAMPIONSHIP DECIDER AGAINST IRELAND AT LANSDOWNE ROAD, DUBLIN. 30/03/2003

BRIAN O'DRISCOLL REACHES OVER TO SCORE IRELAND'S FIRST TRY AGAINST AUSTRALIA DURING THE POOL A MATCH OF THE RUGBY WORLD CUP. 01/11/2003

JASON ROBINSON CELEBRATES SCORING HIS TRY FOR ENGLAND AGAINST AUSTRALIA DURING THE RUGBY WORLD CUP
FINAL AT THE TELSTRA STADIUM, SYDNEY, AUSTRALIA. 22/11/2003

ENGLAND'S JONNY WILKINSON KICKS THE WINNING DROP GOAL TO CLINCH THE RUGBY WORLD CUP FOR ENGLAND IN THE FINAL SECONDS OF A THRILLING FINAL BETWEEN AUSTRALIA AND ENGLAND. 22/11/2003

AUSTRALIA'S JUSTIN HARRISON HOLDS HIS HEAD FOLLOWING DEFEAT IN THE RUGBY WORLD CUP FINAL AGAINST
ENGLAND. 22/11/2003

IRELAND'S CAPTAIN BRIAN O'DRISCOLL (C) IS EMBRACED BY TEAMMATE KEVIN MAGGS WATCHED BY MALCOLM O'KELLY (L) AFTER THEIR RBS 6 NATIONS MATCH AGAINST SCOTLAND AT LANSDOWNE ROAD, DUBLIN. 27/03/2004

BRITISH & IRISH LIONS CAPTAIN BRIAN O'DRISCOLL (C) ACCEPTS THE HAKA CHALLENGE FROM THE ALL BLACKS. 25/06/2005

BRITISH & IRISH LIONS' LEWIS MOODY LEAVES THE PITCH AS NEW ZEALAND CELEBRATE THEIR 48-18 VICTORY. 02/07/2005

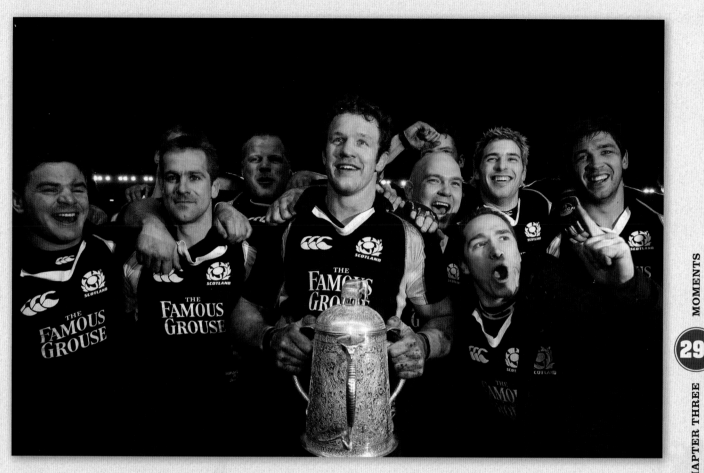

SCOTLAND CAPTAIN JASON WHITE AND HIS TEAMMATES CELEBRATE WITH THE CALCUTTA CUP. 25/02/2006

AUSTRALIA'S CHRIS LATHAM CELEBRATES HIS TRY AGAINST WALES DURING THE INTERNATIONAL MATCH AT THE MILLENENNIUM STADIUM, CARDIFF. 04/11/2006

ENGLAND'S CHARLIE HODGSON IN THE INVESTEC CHALLENGE SERIES AGAINST NEW ZEALAND
AT TWICKENHAM. 05/11/2006

IRELAND'S BRIAN O'DRISCOLL LOOKS AT THE BOARD AFTER ITALY SCORE A LATE TRY DURING THE RBS 6 NATIONS
MATCH AT THE STADIO FLAMINIO, ROME, ITALY. 17/03/2007

IRELAND HOLD A TEAM HUDDLE DURING THE RBS 6 NATIONS MATCH AT THE STADIO FLAMINIO, ROME, ITALY. 17/03/2007

ENGLAND'S PHIL VICKERY CELEBRATES WITH THE CALCUTTA CUP. 03/02/2007

OPPOSITE

ITALY'S MIRCO BERGAMASCO AND SERGIO PARISSE CELEBRATE THEIR TEAM'S
23-20 VICTORY OVER WALES DURING THE RBS 6 NATIONS MATCH AT THE STADIO
FLAMINIO, ROME. 10/03/2007

ENGLAND'S MARK REGAN CELEBRATES AT THE END OF THE IRB RUGBY WORLD CUP SEMI FINAL AGAINST FRANCE AT STADE DE FRANCE. 13/10/2007

SOUTH AFRICA CELEBRATE THEIR VICTORY AGAINST ENGLAND IN THE IRB RUGBY WORLD CUP FINAL MATCH AT STADE DE FRANCE. 20/10/2007

The Publishers gratefully acknowledge PA Photos, from whose extensive archive – including The Press Association, Barratts and Sport & General collections – the photographs in this book have been selected.

Personal copies of the photographs in this book, and many others, may be ordered online at www.prints.paphotos.com

For more information, please contact:

AMMONITE PRESS

AE Publications Ltd. 166 High Street, Lewes, East Sussex, BN7 1XU, United Kingdom

Tel: 01273 488005 Fax: 01273 402866

www.ae-publications.com